Snowy Days of Christmas

New Inspirations of Favorite Carols for Late Intermediate Pianists

Linda Martinez

CONTENTS

PAGE

Music production: **Thomas J. Halm**
Cover design: **Susan H. Hartman**
Cover photos: **PhotoDisc**

ISBN-10: 0-7390-2965-7
ISBN-13: 978-0-7390-2965-7

Hark! The Herald Angels Sing

Felix Mendelssohn

arr. Linda Martinez

15
mf
18
f
21
poco rit.
a tempo
mf
24
f
p
mp
27

30
32
molto rit.
34
Majestically
a tempo
ff
36
38

40
43
mp
46
poco rit.
a tempo
f
48
50
poco rit.
mp

Away in a Manger

W.J. Kirkpatrick
arr. Linda Martinez

a tempo
poco rit.
13
p
16
mp
19
mf
22
f
25

28
poco rit.
31
a tempo
34
38
43
simile

47
2
1
51
poco rit.
a tempo
54
p
57
60
poco rit.

I Saw Three Ships

Traditional English
arr. Linda Martinez

Brightly (♩. = 120)

13
16
19
22
25
simile
subito p

27
f
mf
30
simile
33
36
p
simile
39

42
molto rit.
a tempo
f
ff
simile
45
48
51
p
54

O Come, O Come, Emmanuel

Traditional

arr. Linda Martinez

22
27
31
34
37

41
mf
44
48
f
53
mp
p
59
mf

65
p
71
77
mf
p
82
mf
p
87
poco rit.
pp

The First Noel

Traditional English

arr. Linda Martinez

Sweetly (♩= 92)

17
21
24
27
30

33
36
39
f
42
45

48
p
51
f
mp
55
58
61
f

64
rit.
ff
8vb
67
a tempo
p
71
74
77
pp

Oh Christmas Tree

Traditional German
arr. Linda Martinez

Energetically! (♩=110)

13
15
f
17
19
subito mp
21
mf

23
f
p
25
28
mf
31
33

35
37
f
39
41
43
p

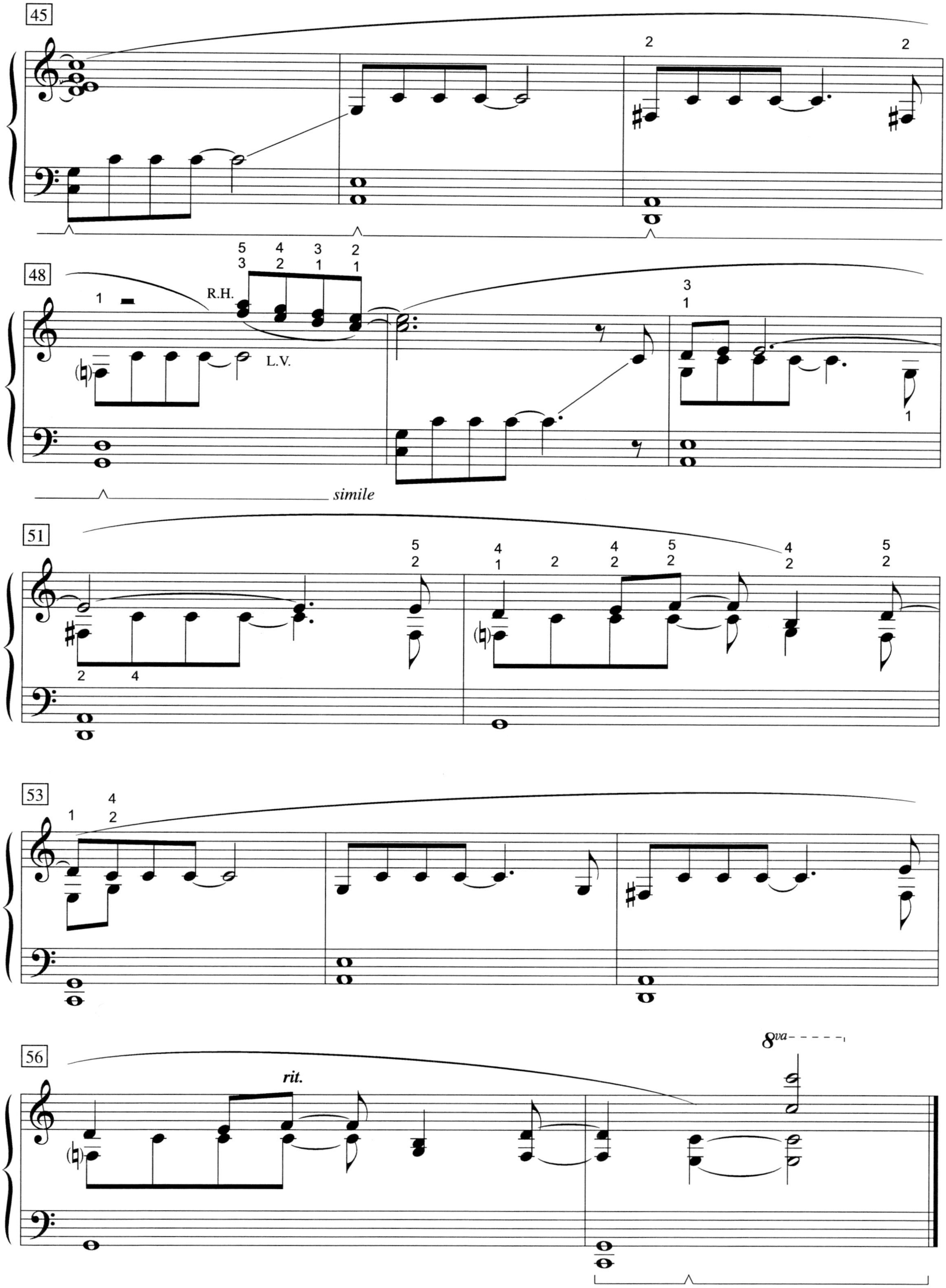
45
48
R.H.
L.V.
simile
51
53
56
rit.
8va

The Coventry Carol

Traditional

arr. Linda Martinez

10
12
14
16
18
f
p
molto f

20
subito p
f
23
piu mosso
p
27
31
rit.
a tempo I
f
simile
33
subito p

35
37
39
f
41
mp
44
p

About the Arranger

LINDA MARTINEZ

Composer, Pianist

Linda Martinez was born in Whittier, California in 1975. She began her musical training under the auspices of the Yamaha Music Education Center in La Mirada at the age of four. She was composing by age six and by age eight was performing her original music nationwide including concerts at the Kennedy Center and the United Nations. Though her early performance background was strictly classical, she later turned to studying and performing jazz, winning the 1992 Los Angeles Music Center Spotlight Award and the 1993 Los Angeles Jazz Society Shelly Manne Award for New Talent. She was also the U.S. winner and representative to Japan in 1991, performing her jazz sextet *Gunther and I* at the Yamaha International Junior Original Concert Composition Competition in Tokyo. Linda is now an artist and clinician for Yamaha's piano, keyboard, and education divisions.

After completing her studies in composition at the University of Southern California in 1998, she returned to performing as a keyboardist for the Fox Television Network late night show *The Keenen Ivory Wayans Show,* leading to performances with other artists such as *Genuine, Jagged Edge, Crystal,* and *Sugar Ray.* In 2000, she began touring with *Destiny's Child* and has worked closely with music director Robert Bacon to orchestrate and produce their live shows, including the 2001 Grammy Awards, the 2001 Brit Awards, and the 2001 MTV Icon Awards honoring Janet Jackson. She most recently composed and produced original instrumental music for their 2001 MTV TRL Independent Women tour. She is currently the assistant to four-time Emmy Award-winning film composer Laura Karpman, scoring additional music and performing on many of her scores, including Columbia/Tri Star's *The Princess and the Marine,* PBS's award-winning *The Living Edens, Egypt: Beyond the Pyramids* for the History Channel, *Surviving Gilligan's Island* for CBS, and *Woman of Independent Means* produced by Sally Field.